BLM

The BLM NEVADA
NATIONAL LANDSCAPE CONSERVATION SYSTEM
Strategy

On March 30, 2009, President Barack Obama signed the Omnibus Public Land Management Act, which states: "In order to conserve, protect, and restore nationally significant landscapes that have outstanding cultural, ecological, and scientific values for the benefit of current and future generations, there is established in the Bureau of Land Management the National Landscape Conservation System." [Sec. 2002 (a)] "The Secretary shall manage the system in accordance with any applicable law (including regulations) relating to any component of the system...and in a manner that protects the values for which the components of the system were designated." [Sec. 2002 (c)]

Dear Friends of the BLM Nevada,

I am pleased to share this new plan, our strategy for managing Nevada's National Landscape Conservation System lands. These lands represent some of the most scenic, culturally rich, and scientifically important of all public lands in the State.

BLM Nevada manages three national conservation areas: Black Rock Desert-High Rock Canyon, Red Rock Canyon and Sloan Canyon; 45 wilderness areas; 63 wilderness study areas and three national historic trails.

We are committed to responsibly managing these lands and this strategy document is an important step towards achieving BLM Nevada's goal of conserving these areas.

We would like to thank all of the partners and BLM employees who help us manage these special conservation lands and have contributed to this document. We are also grateful to the many photographers who assisted us with artwork. This strategy would not be complete without your contributions.

Sincerely,

Amy Lueders
BLM Nevada State Director

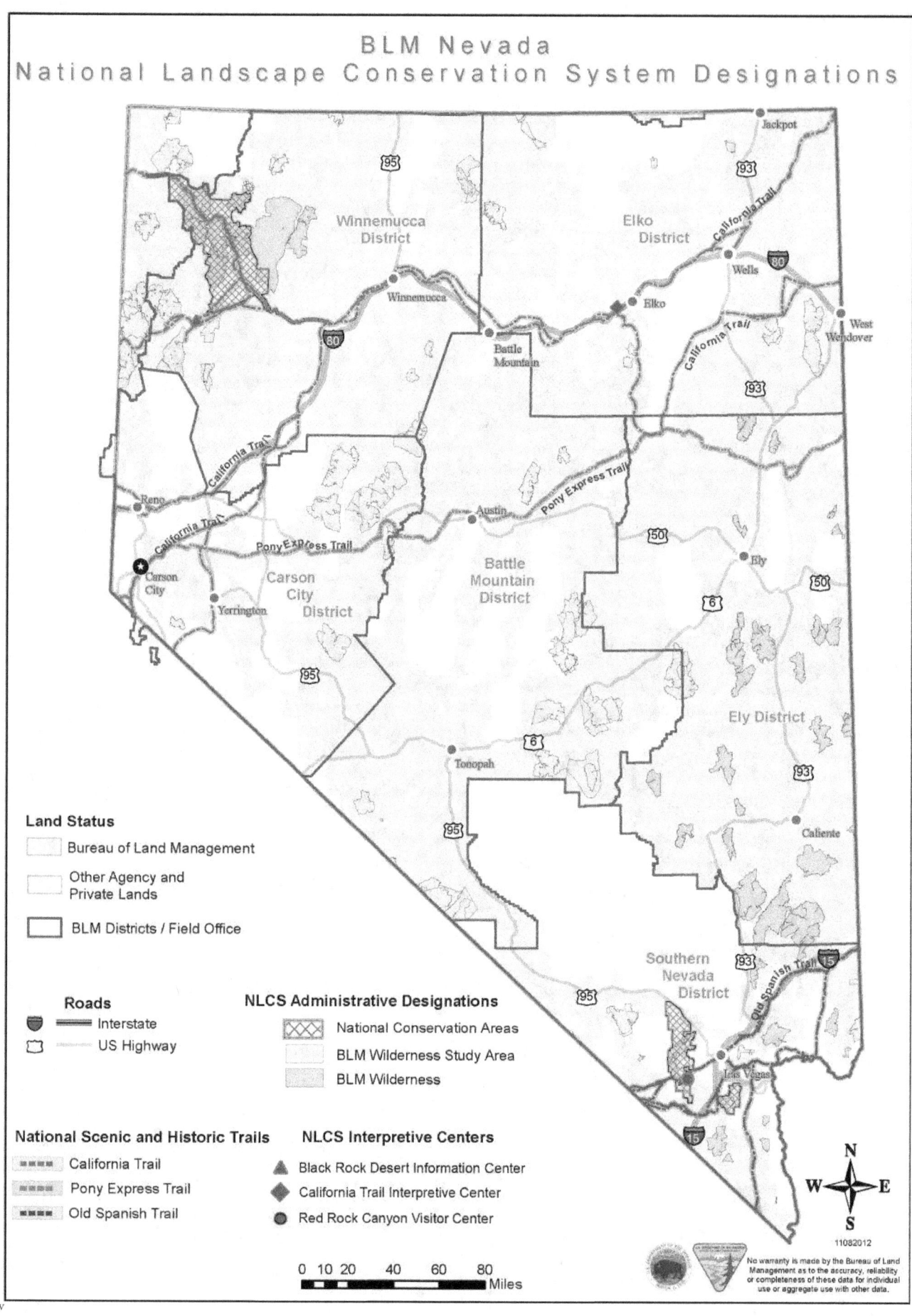

BLM Nevada
National Landscape Conservation System Designations

Land Status

Bureau of Land Management

Other Agency and Private Lands

BLM Districts / Field Office

Roads

Interstate

US Highway

NLCS Administrative Designations

National Conservation Areas

BLM Wilderness Study Area

BLM Wilderness

National Scenic and Historic Trails

California Trail

Pony Express Trail

Old Spanish Trail

NLCS Interpretive Centers

▲ Black Rock Desert Information Center

◆ California Trail Interpretive Center

● Red Rock Canyon Visitor Center

0 10 20 40 60 80 Miles

N
W E
S

11082012

No warranty is made by the Bureau of Land Management as to the accuracy, reliability or completeness of these data for individual use or aggregate use with other data.

iv

"Those who haven't the strength or youth to go into it... can simply contemplate the idea, take pleasure in the fact that such a timeless and uncontrolled part of earth is still there.... We simply need that wild country available to us, even if we never do more than drive to its edge and look in. For it can be a means of reassuring ourselves of our sanity as creatures, a part of the geography of hope."

Wallace Stegner, "The Sound of Mountain Water"

Hedgehog Cactus, Black Velvet Canyon Photo by Chelsie Simmons

Mission and Vision for the National Landscape Conservation System (NLCS)

The Bureau of Land Management's (BLM) mission for the NLCS is to conserve, protect, and restore nationally significant landscapes and places that have outstanding cultural, ecological, and scientific values for the benefit of current and future generations.

The BLM's vision for the NLCS is to be a world leader in conservation by protecting landscapes, applying evolving knowledge, and bringing people together to share stewardship of the land.

Components of the NLCS

As defined by the Omnibus Public Land Management Act of 2009, the NLCS includes the following areas administered by the BLM:

- National Monuments

- National Conservation Areas

- Components of the National Wilderness Preservation System

- Wilderness Study Areas

- Components of the National Wild and Scenic Rivers System

- National Scenic Trails or National Historic Trails Designated as Components of the National Trails System

- Any area designated by Congress to be administered for conservation purposes.

Nevada is a beautiful state that offers endless panoramic vistas that stretch as far as the eye can see, and countless experiences and opportunities for those seeking unique outdoor adventures. Endowed with approximately 48 million acres of nationally significant resources, the Bureau of Land Management (BLM) Nevada has many special designations which are part of the National Landscape Conservation System (NLCS), also referred to as BLM's "National Conservation Lands".

Our employees, partners, stakeholders and volunteers work cooperatively to manage NLCS lands and resources, provide visitor information and services, conduct scientific monitoring and analysis, promote recreation opportunities and complete resource enhancement projects. The statewide map shows the locations of these extraordinary conservation lands and resources.

In order to ensure the conservation, protection, and restoration of these NLCS units, the BLM developed a 15-year national strategy in 2012 entitled "The Geography of Hope." Each state was asked to develop its own strategy tiered to this national guidance to conserve, protect, and restore lands and resources within NLCS units. This document will help guide BLM Nevada's NLCS program for the next five years.

The National and Nevada strategies follow four basic Themes. Each Theme is supported by Goals that further refine BLM Nevada's strategic approach to managing NLCS units. The State Level Action items are listed under each goal. Field Level Actions, which identify specific on-the-ground projects to meet the Goals of the strategy are available at www.blm.gov/nv. The Field Level Actions will be updated on an annual basis by each Field Office that has NLCS units.

Top: Reno Chapter Backcountry Horsemen Horsepacking in High Rock Canyon Photo by Paula Lenz

Bottom: Mormon Mountain Wilderness Photo by Jani Ahlvers

Red Rock Canyon Moon Photo by David Klinger

BLM Nevada's NLCS Units

At this time, Nevada's NLCS units consist of three National Conservation Areas (NCAs), 45 wilderness areas, 63 wilderness study areas (WSAs), and three National Historic Trails (NHTs).

National Conservation Areas

BLM Nevada's three NCAs total more than one million acres.

Black Rock Desert-High Rock Canyon Emigrant Trails NCA, in northwestern Nevada, was primarily established to protect and preserve the unique and nationally significant historic trail corridors and the associated viewsheds that emigrants experienced on their difficult journeys across the west. The Applegate-Lassen Trail and Nobles Trail corridors and surrounding areas contain portions of John C. Fremont's 1843-1844 exploration route through the Great Basin. Outstanding biological resources are also a part of this NLCS unit.

Red Rock Canyon NCA, in southern Nevada, contains unique natural and cultural resources that stand in stark contrast to the nearby city of Las Vegas. More than one million visitors enjoy Red Rock Canyon's scenic beauty each year. Highlights of the NCA include a 13-mile Scenic Backcountry Byway with views of a spectacular 1500 foot high sandstone escarpment. There is also a visitor center and more than 30 miles of hiking and biking trails. Other recreation uses include sightseeing, rock climbing, birding, and horseback riding.

Sloan Canyon NCA, also in southern Nevada, contains one of the most significant prehistoric rock art sites in Nevada. It is 20 miles southeast of Las Vegas, bordering the City of Henderson, in the northern portion of the McCullough Range. There are more than 300 rock art panels with over 1,700 individual design elements created by Native Americans over thousands of years. Primary recreation uses include hiking, mountain biking and horseback riding.

"Supreme overall is the silence. Discounting the cry of the occasional bird, the wailing of a pack of coyotes, silence-a great spatial silence-is pure in the basin and range."

John McPhee

Pahute Peak Wilderness Photo by Brian Beffort

WILDERNESS AND WILDERNESS STUDY AREAS

As of 2012, the BLM Nevada's 45 wilderness areas total 2,055,005 acres. Wilderness areas are intended to be essentially undisturbed by human activity. These areas will be managed in perpetuity in accordance with the Wilderness Act of 1964 and the Bureau's wilderness management regulations.

BLM Nevada continues to manage 63 WSAs totaling 2,552,387 acres. These areas are actively administered to ensure that wilderness values are preserved and protected until such time as Congress decides either to designate these areas as wilderness or release them for multiple-use purposes.

National Historic Trails

BLM Nevada manages three NHTs: California NHT, Pony Express NHT, and Old Spanish NHT. The California Trail, located in northern Nevada, stretches across 700 miles of BLM-managed land. The recently opened California Trail Interpretive Center near Elko interprets the history of this trail. The Pony Express Trail crosses 300 miles of central Nevada. Several Pony Express stations are part of the history of this trail and can be visited by the public. The Old Spanish Trail, in southern Nevada, stretches across 125 miles of BLM managed lands, and includes portions of the original 1820's-era mule route, as well as a later wagon route established by Mormon pioneers.

Facilities, Visitor and Interpretive Centers

Red Rock Canyon Visitor Center, California Trail Interpretive Center and Black Rock Station Administrative Facility are vitally important for sharing information with visitors from around the world. The State will continue trying to obtain additional base funds for these facilities. Each unit is encouraged to work with their local communities and partners to assist in maintaining and improving these facilities for current and future visitors.

At this time we do not manage any Wild and Scenic Rivers.

Go to www.blm.gov/nv for copies of the legislation for each NCA and the California Trail Center.

THE FUTURE

While discussing the strategy and its four themes with our partners, we realized each theme is equally important and interconnected, thus on-going communication with our partners and the public is crucial to achieving the goals of the strategy.

Future additional funding will be directed towards the types of projects identified in this strategy and field level plans.

Red Rock Canyon Photo by Jacob Klein

"One cannot be pessimistic about the West. This is the native home of hope. When it fully learns that cooperation, not rugged individualism, is the quality that most characterizes and preserves it, then it will have achieved itself and outlived its origins. Then it has a chance to create a society to match its scenery."

Wallace Stegner, "The Sound of Mountain Water"

NLCS Strategy Themes and Goals

This strategy reflects the best of the ideas and suggestions offered by the public and BLM employees and incorporates the requirements of Secretarial Order 3308 (Appendix 2), the America's Great Outdoors Report, the Department of the Interior Strategic Plan for 2011-2016, and other sources. The result is a strategy that is integrated and interdisciplinary in nature, will assist in NLCS budget development in the coming years, and will help the BLM determine what work is most important within individual NLCS units.

Jackson Mountains Wilderness Area Photo by Brian Murdock

Theme 1	***Ensuring the Conservation, Protection, and Restoration of NLCS Values.*** Primacy of conservation within the NLCS, how science serves to further conservation, and to provide for compatible use that protects NLCS resources and values.
Theme 2	***Collaboratively Managing the NLCS as Part of the Larger Landscape.*** Building a better conservation model through collaborative management.
Theme 3	***Raising Awareness of the Value and Benefits of the BLM's NLCS.*** Raise public awareness and understanding of the NLCS, cultivate relationships, promote community stewardship of BLM-managed public land, and provide for use and enjoyment of present and future generations.
Theme 4	***Building upon BLM's Commitment to Conservation.*** Promote a model of conservation excellence internally, through improved understanding and fully integrating the NLCS within the BLM.

Theme 1	*Ensuring the Conservation, Protection, and Restoration of NLCS Values*

The NLCS lands are designated by Congress or the President to conserve, protect, and restore their unique values for the benefit of current and future generations. As such, there is an overarching and explicit commitment to conservation and resource protection as the primary objective within these areas. In this theme, we focus on ensuring that BLM management of NLCS lands is guided by the purposes for which the lands were designated and on using science to further conservation, protection, and restoration of these landscapes, while providing opportunities for compatible public use and enjoyment.

Goal 1A

Clearly communicate that the conservation, protection, and restoration of NLCS values is the highest priority in NLCS planning and management, consistent with the designating legislation or presidential proclamation.

1. Increase our knowledge of the natural and cultural environment. Share research, scientific findings and monitoring efforts with the public.

2. Implement management plans for NLCS units as funding permits. Focus management emphasis on completing projects identified through planning efforts.

3. Ensure serialized case files, including boundary descriptions, are kept current.

4. Maintain an effective system of directional and information signs that are consistent in appearance, while minimizing visual impacts to the surrounding environment. Replace or repair all deficient directional signs in all units.

5. Highlight conservation, protection and restoration actions to enhance values within the NLCS units. Promote and publicize accomplishments to the public, user groups and NV Resource Advisory Councils (RACs).

Goal 1B

Expand understanding of the NLCS values through assessment, inventory, and monitoring.

1. Complete and maintain up to date inventories of resource values at NLCS units and incorporate into management and implementation plans. Assess the integrity of resource conditions and values. Use the described unit values to provide a clear focus for statewide priority assessments of proposed management and restoration projects.

2. Utilize and improve the integration of existing Resource Assessments for NCA Decision Making. Examples include: Land Health Assessments, Appropriate Management Level (AML) evaluations, water and forage utilization monitoring; travel management inventories, etc.

3. Incorporate long term wildlife data accrued by the Nevada Department of Wildlife. Promote partnerships with organizations and NGOs to enhance inventory efforts.

4. Complete wilderness characteristics inventories and update as necessary.

5. Promote vegetation management, restoration, and fuels reduction projects where appropriate to reduce the risk of wildfire and promote healthy and diverse plant communities in NLCS units.

6. Develop and maintain a geodatabase to manage data and spatially display projects on Nevada NLCS units.

7. Monitor site conditions at cultural sites to assess risk to heritage resources.

8. Encourage subject matter experts to share their knowledge with the public to increase awareness of the diverse programs within the BLM.

Goal 1C

Provide a scientific foundation for decision-making.

1. Encourage interdisciplinary project proposals that incorporate multiple resource values and are mutually compatible. Enter these projects into the BLM Budget Planning System (BPS).

2. Support and promote research activities consistent with the protection of National Conservation Lands in order to further knowledge and understanding of the natural and cultural resources of the NLCS units.

3. Integrate science into management plans to assist in decision making and identify research needs.

4. Develop partnerships with universities and conservation groups to increase baseline data collection and develop science/research projects to promote science-based decision making.

Goal 1D

Use the NLCS as an outdoor laboratory and demonstration center for new and innovative management and business processes that aid in the conservation, protection, and restoration of NLCS areas.

1. Encourage funding requests and support submissions that further our scientific knowledge. Encourage interdisciplinary project proposals that cross cut resource values and are mutually compatible. Seek outside grants and other alternative sources for additional funding that further our scientific knowledge in NLCS units.

2. Develop innovative methods to reclaim surface disturbances, remove unauthorized structures and developments to further conservation, protection, and restoration of wilderness values within designated wilderness and WSAs.

Goal 1E

Limit discretionary uses to those compatible with the conservation, protection, and restoration of the values for which NLCS lands were designated.

1. Continue to implement management plans for each NLCS unit. Engage interested publics, Resource Advisory Councils (RACs), Tribal, State and local governments during the development of management plans. Identify potential conflicts and work with stakeholders to resolve conflicts before significant investment of resources in projects.

2. Use resource information available in other assessments, such as Rapid Ecological Assessments and Resource Management Plans when determining applicable types of discretionary uses.

3. Prepare management plans for designated wilderness areas.

4. Use the principles of the BLM National Historic Trails manuals to establish and manage National Historic Trail corridors.

5. Ensure all employees that work in NLCS understand the legislation, BLM Policy and manuals for the units they are working in.

Goal 1F

Manage facilities in a manner that conserves, protects, and restores NLCS values.

1. Continue to work with local communities and partners to assist with staffing and obtain alternative funding to help leverage BLM's costs to operate facilities.

2. Encourage the development of visitor centers on non-federal lands within local communities to build stewardship, contribute to the local economy and provide for public safety and enjoyment.

3. Minimize development of facilities on BLM lands to help preserve the natural resources and ensure that improvements to existing facilities improve and manage access to sustainable recreation opportunities and protecting the area's resources.

Red Springs Boardwalk Trail, Red Rock Canyon Photo by Alan O'Neill

Theme 2 | Collaboratively Managing the NLCS as Part of the Larger Landscape

Recognizing that the NLCS represents a small portion of the land managed by the BLM and other federal, state, tribal, and local government entities, these special conservation areas must be managed within the context of the larger landscape. By establishing connections across boundaries with other jurisdictions, management of NLCS areas will complement conservation areas within the respective jurisdictions of the National Park Service, the Fish and Wildlife Service Refuge System, the U.S. Forest Service, state and local governments, private conservation lands, and other BLM land managed for resource protection through land-use plan designations.

Collaborative management is also a major theme in the President's America's Great Outdoors (AGO) Report published February 2011. The BLM is implementing various AGO actions that will further enhance management of NLCS and other BLM lands, such as serving on the America's Great Outdoors Federal Interagency Council on Outdoor Recreation to coordinate recreation management, access, and policies across multiple agencies. Finally, taking a collaborative landscape approach to NLCS management provides better opportunities to promote healthy landscapes and contribute to the local economy and social fabric of the community.

Goal 2A

Emphasize an ecosystem-based approach to manage the NLCS in the context of the surrounding landscape.

1.   Collaborate and manage NLCS lands within the context of larger landscape efforts, such as the Regional Ecosystem Assessment, Assessment Inventory and Monitoring Strategy, and Healthy Landscapes within the Great Basin and Mojave Desert of Nevada.

2.   Develop and implement educational materials/programs that focus on the long-term benefits of healthy resources.

Black Rock Point Photo by Ambrose Krouse

3. Provide visitor information on the fragility of desert environments.

4. Ensure non-native invasive plant assessments and weed eradication within designated wilderness and WSAs remain a statewide priority.

Goal 2B

Adopt a cross-jurisdictional, community-based approach to landscape-level conservation planning and management.

1. Coordinate across all BLM Programs and partners/stakeholders to leverage resources such as volunteers, time, funding, staff hours and equipment.

2. Encourage community based partnerships with local governments, partners and/or private entities, to locate future visitor infrastructure in the gateway communities. This will assist with economic development of local communities while conserving and preserving NLCS resources.

3. Encourage and support the development of Conservation Easements with willing private landowners where such actions will benefit wildlife, watershed and cultural resources and other uses.

4. Submit parcels for Land and Water Conservation Fund dollars to acquire inholdings when there is a willing seller.

5. Prepare management plans for designated wilderness areas.

6. Continue to partner with the National Park Service trail preservation groups and neighboring states to ensure consistent and effective cross-jurisdictional conservation planning and management of National Historic Trails.

Goal 2C

Work with Congress, Tribes, other federal and state agencies, and national and local communities to identify and protect lands that are critical to the long-term ecological sustainability of the landscape.

1. Work with Tribes, state and county agencies in preparing resource management and implementation level land use planning documents.

2. Engage Tribes on traditional uses of subsistence resources and match native seed collection and planting by the BLM to these uses to the extent possible.

3. Work with other agencies and local communities to determine ecological sustainability for each area.

Goal 2D

Adopt a community-based approach to recreation and visitor services delivery, consistent with the conservation purpose of the NLCS and the socio-economic goals of the local community.

1. Implement regional cooperative approaches to promote domestic and international tourism and to provide sustainable recreational opportunities and visitor services that enhance the natural and cultural heritage of a region and contribute to the local economy. To the extent feasible, utilize existing collaborative forums or regional recreation planning efforts.

2. Encourage partnering in the development and management of visitor and interpretive centers, facilities, and services in gateway communities in order to provide "one-stop shopping" for visitors and tell the story of the landscape and the community. Conduct periodic visitor surveys to assess visitor satisfaction and identify visitor needs.

3. More actively promote use of collaborative/cooperative law enforcement agreements with other federal, state and local agencies to bring in trained auxiliary rangers to provide visitor safety, protect resources, deter criminal activities, and investigate and prosecute crime.

Theme 3 | Raising Awareness of the Value and Benefits of the BLM's NLCS

This theme seeks to cultivate a sense of shared stewardship for the BLM-managed public lands and advance the relevance of conservation lands to communities of place and interest. The goals represent a multi-pronged approach to connect diverse groups of people, interests, and government organizations by building strong partnerships, attracting volunteers, engaging youth, and telling our story through education, interpretation, and outreach.

Goal 3A

Launch a long-term public awareness initiative about the BLM Nevada's NLCS, including national and local outreach, communications, and media plans.

1.   Develop and implement a communications plan to highlight NLCS units. This plan will be part of a larger strategic communications plan for the state.

2.   Coordinate with the Nevada Commission on Tourism, and the local Convention and Visitor's Authorities, regarding Brand USA and marketing those NLCS units where increased visitation is consistent with protection of resource values and the management plans for the unit.

3.   Develop a collection of photographs and articles which will be used to emphasize the value of NLCS units and the opportunities available to promote resource enhancement, recreation, volunteer, etc. Include these success stories on BLM NV web pages, social media and as part of a (resurrected) statewide external newsletter.

4.   Emphasize the use of electronics, such as social media, web pages, podcasts, etc. to provide information about volunteer and recreation opportunities offered by BLM Nevada.

5.   Use the NLCS visitor/interpretive centers to disseminate information for their area of the state and to help increase awareness of the BLM and its multiple use mission.

Black Rock National Public Lands Day Photo by Brian Beffort

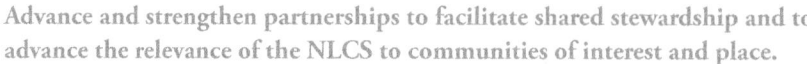

Goal 3B

Advance and strengthen partnerships to facilitate shared stewardship and to advance the relevance of the NLCS to communities of interest and place.

1. Work with friends groups and partners for further outreach to boost recognition and community support for BLM Nevada and its NLCS sites.

2. Continue to build upon our network of existing partners. Develop an umbrella group under which this network can function to try to secure additional funding through alternate sources (both internal and external). Encourage partners to become more economically self-sustaining.

3. The Grants and Agreements Office will continue to assist and train BLM staff and partners about partnerships and update the Agreements Sharepoint Site to help provide information for employees.

4. Invite our partners to the 2014 Recreation, NLCS, Wilderness Workshop.

5. Provide information and guidance regarding the Challenge Cost Share Program to both partners and employees including assisting partners with ideas on how to acquire the 1:1 match.

6. Work with partners and off-highway vehicle groups to assist with resource monitoring activities, rehabilitation and restoration projects.

7. Follow the guidance in the BLM Partnership Strategy which will be distributed in 2013.

Goal 3C

Expand use of volunteers within the NLCS.

1. Identify and market programs and projects where volunteer assistance would be necessary and desirable.

2. Provide opportunities for volunteers to work alongside scientists, researchers and other BLM specialists.

3. Develop and implement projects with partners and volunteers for special events such as National Public Lands Day.

4. Develop a BLM Nevada annual volunteer recognition award. Honor exemplary volunteers by submitting their names for annual volunteer awards.

5. Highlight noteworthy volunteer accomplishments in news releases, BLM Blast articles and other avenues.

Goal 3D   Engage the public in stewardship of the NLCS through education and interpretation.

1.   Work with partners to further develop and implement innovative education and interpretive programs.

2.   Provide staff and partners with the training and contact information to develop innovative outreach methods and enhance outreach programs.

3.   Continue proactive law enforcement actions helping to provide visitor information and education about the value and importance of National Conservation Lands.

4.   Develop Junior Explorer Books and Student Activity Books, and on-line resources for teachers.

5.   Resource and Public Affairs Specialists will coordinate development of outreach materials to disseminate research findings to the general public. This would include online information, booklets, interpretive panels and presentations.

6.   Follow the guidance in the BLM Education, Interpretation and Youth Strategy which will be distributed in 2013.

Goal 3E   Recruit and retain well-trained youth from diverse backgrounds for entry-level careers, and engage youth in recreation, education, and stewardship on conservation lands.

1.   Emphasize youth employment opportunities. Focus on nurturing students and youth toward seeking permanent careers in natural resources management. Include partnerships with tribes to develop employment opportunities.

2.   Whenever possible, dedicate one-time youth hiring funding to NLCS units.

3.   Offer academic internships at NLCS units. Specifically target programs that require an internship for graduation.

4.   Plan and sponsor at least one project a year at the California Trail Center and each NCA utilizing a youth intern.

5.   Use the Veteran's Employment Program to recruit qualified veterans.

6.   Work with local schools and universities to attend job fairs which inform students of hiring opportunities.

Goal 3F

Engage youth in appreciation of the natural environment through both formal and informal settings. Include the use of family-oriented programs, as well as school, tribal, and youth group programs. Use social networking and other current technologies to deliver messages and experiences. Programs that capture youth early can lead to future interest in careers in natural resource management. Tie into "Let's Move Outside" initiative where opportunities exist.

1. Expand Hands on the Land sites so that one site is tied to each national conservation area.

2. Work with partners to Initiate and expand elementary through high school programs and other youth group programs, such as Indoor/Outdoor classrooms.

3. Establish partnerships with colleges or universities to provide field schools and or youth camp opportunities on NLCS units.

4. Provide NLCS information for existing teacher education programs, such as Project Archaeology and other CEUs. Work with local universities and school districts to develop additional related curriculum.

5. Encourage all offices to plan projects which include physical activity and include them as "Let's Move Outside" projects.

Goal 3G

Utilize youth groups as a ready source of community-minded young citizens eager to provide assistance in management of public lands. Seek out citizen-based family groups that organize recreation and outdoor opportunities on NLCS properties. Providing and expanding on these opportunities on NLCS units introduces youth to stewardship ethics and ownership in these special places.

1. Provide partner opportunities for youth groups and clubs such as: Boy Scouts, Girl Scouts, 4-H Clubs, etc.

2. Provide outreach information and participate in special events at retail stores that specialize in outdoor gear.

Above: Americorps interns leading a youth hike in the Black Rock Desert.

Left: Performers at the California Trail Center.

Conservation

This theme outlines goals and actions to improve internal communication and facilitate intra-agency coordination in a way that aligns and fully integrates the NLCS program within the BLM.

Goal 4A

Increase internal communication and understanding of the NLCS lands in NV and its potential to enhance the BLM as a whole.

1. Develop and implement an internal Communication Plan which will include information about NLCS units. This will be part of a larger strategic communications plan for the state that educates BLM employees about the place of National Conservation Lands within the BLM organization.

2. Write feature articles about interesting things happening on NLCS lands. Post these articles on the social media sites.

3. Each NCA will be encouraged to develop and implement an environmental education and outreach plan that meets teachers' needs which will highlight resource protection, the values of NLCS, etc.

4. Provide the following internal opportunities: Feature NLCS as an agenda item at State Leadership Team (SLT) meetings; Have NLCS as a topic in any new employee orientation; Discuss NLCS at BLM program workshops

5. Encourage employees to participate in training modules produced by the National Training Center (NTC).

6. Pilot a project to develop mobile applications for each NCA and the California Trail Center.

7. Field Managers will continue to share NLCS information with the District and Field Office staffs at District Leadership Team and All Employee Meetings.

Goal 4B

Cultivate shared responsibility for the NLCS conservation mandate as an integral part of BLM's multiple-use, sustained-yield mission.

1. Work closely with the NLCS units, State Director's Office and the Washington Office to ensure policies and strategies are implemented in a consistent manner.

2. Ensure all employees and major partners plan work that compliments NLCS unit objectives and values.

3. Ensure all employees have access to a copy of the NLCS Strategy and are aware of their responsibilities in implementing NLCS policy.

4. Ensure potential conflicts between any NLCS policy and other program management are resolved.

5. Encourage BLM employees with non NLCS duties to serve on details in offices with NLCS units.

Goal 4C

Clearly define, understand, and justify staffing needs, and administratively organize the NLCS areas to operate as a cross-cutting program within the BLM.

1. Ensure NLCS is always included in any target organization exercise. Each NCA has a core staff but must also rely on the expertise of other program specialists from their respective District Offices. Non NLCS employees can be directed to use their regularly allocated program funding within NLCS units when completing work in those areas.

2. Have NLCS as a topic in any new employee orientations; discuss at pertinent program workshops.

3. NSO Office of Law Enforcement will continue to submit BPS proposals to obtain additional law enforcement officers to enhance visitor safety and protect the fragile archeological, paleontological and biological treasures within the NLCS units.

Goal 4D

Ensure the NLCS budget and associated workload targets are coordinated with the other BLM programs. Set clear expectations and procedures for interdisciplinary budget development, priority setting, and reporting of accomplishments.

1. Work with local communities and friends groups to come up with innovative ways to raise funds to assist with labor and operations and other maintenance costs.

2. Ensure NCA budget submissions are consistent with actions described in each NCA's current implementation plan.

3. Coordinate interdisciplinary initiatives to obtain additional funding for necessary projects and personnel. This includes encouraging offices to develop NLCS research proposals and Challenge Cost Share projects with partners.

4. Develop a procedure so Field Managers can require prior authorization of purchases in the Recreation Fees (1232) and Cost Recovery (5105) fund codes.

5. Each NLCS unit which charges a fee, or collects donations, will develop a business plan which will be approved by the State Director's Office.

6. Develop innovative ideas to fund visitor/interpretive centers. All visitor/interpretive centers are encouraged to develop additional partnerships to manage the facility and programs.

7. Use concession leases where it would be more feasible to have an outside entity manage the activity/facility, etc.

8. Submit BPS projects in the appropriate centrally funded initiatives to try to obtain additional funds.

9. Submit unfunded priorities when necessary to try to obtain additional funding.

10. Work with the Engineering Program Lead to obtain as much facility maintenance funding as necessary.

11. Improve the target coordination amongst all the State Office program leads involved with programs involving NLCS.

Photo by Brian Belfort

The Nevada NLCS Strategy is the result of a collaborative effort among BLM managers, staff and partners. Thank you for taking the time to help develop and review this document. Your views and our continuing conversations about resource protection and multiple-use greatly enhanced the strategy.

We also want to thank members of the public for your continued support of the BLM's NLCS and sharing your ideas, photos and drawings. We recognize that this strategy is only the beginning and we look forward to sharing stewardship of this immense, inspiring, and hopeful land.

Kyle Canyon Burros Photo by Eric Thomson

"The beauty of our land is a natural resource. It's preservation is linked to the inner prosperity of the human spirit. The tradition of our past is equal to today's threat to that beauty."

President Lyndon B. Johnson

Red Rock Canyon Photo by Van Phetsomphou

Glossary

AIM: The Assessment, Inventory and Monitoring Strategy for Integrated Renewable Resources Management is a document intended to reach across programs, jurisdictions, stakeholders, and agencies to provide data and information valuable to decision makers. The strategy focuses on 10 management questions impor¬tant to land managers at varying levels of the Bureau, from field office to national levels.

BPS: The Budget Planning System was designed to streamline the BLM's budget process and enable them to compete effectively for a budget that would support their programs and goals.

Citizen Science: A term used for projects or ongoing program of scientific work in which individual volunteers or networks of volunteers, many of whom may have no specific scientific training, perform or manage research-related tasks such as observation, measurement, or computation.

Components of the NLCS:

National Monuments are areas designated for conservation purposes either by act of Congress or presidential proclamation under authority of the 1906 American Antiquities Act.

National Conservation Areas are areas designated for conservation purposes by act of Congress.

Wilderness Areas are part of the National Wilderness Preservation System established by the 1964 Wilderness Act: "*A wilderness, in contrast with those areas where man and his own works dominate the landscape, is hereby recognized as an area where the earth and community of life are untrammeled by man, where man himself is a visitor who does not remain.*" Each addition to the National Wilderness Preservation System is specifically designated by act of Congress. Wilderness areas are managed by the BLM, U.S. Forest Service, National Park Service, and U.S. Fish and Wildlife Service.

Wilderness Study Areas are areas with wilderness characteristics designated through the inventory and study processes authorized by Section 603 of FLPMA prior to 2003, or through the planning process authorized by Section 202 of FLPMA.

Wild and Scenic Rivers are rivers or river sections designated either by act of Congress or through the recommendation of a Governor and administrative action by the Secretary of the Interior. These rivers are designated to preserve their free-flowing condition and are not dammed or otherwise impeded. The National Wild and Scenic Rivers System was established through the National Wild and Scenic Rivers Act of 1968.

National Scenic Trails or National Historic Trails are extended trails designated by act of Congress to protect their natural beauty or historic qualities. National scenic and historic trails are components of the National Trails System authorized through the National Trails System Act of 1968.

Conservation: The harmonious and coordinated management of the various resources without permanent impairment of the productivity of the land and the quality of the environment. (Sec. 103(c) FLPMA)

Cultural Landscapes: Are distinct geographical areas or properties uniquely representing the combined work of nature and of man.

Implementation Plan: Upon approval of the land use plan, subsequent implementation decisions are put into effect by developing implementation (activity-level or project-specific) plans. An activity-level plan typically describes multiple projects in detail that will lead to on-the-ground action. Activity-level plans are increasingly interdisciplinary and are focused on multiple resource program areas to reflect the shift to a more watershed-based or landscape-based approach to management. [BLM H-1601-1 Land Use Planning Handbook, Section IV. A. (March, 2005)]

Implementation Strategy: A useful tool to facilitate successful implementation of land use plans. An implementation strategy lists prioritized decisions that (1) will help achieve the desired outcomes of one or more land use plans and (2) can be implemented given existing or anticipated resources. Developing implementation strategies enables the BLM to prioritize the preparation of implementation decisions. A well thought-out implementation strategy should prioritize each decision for funding and implementation. The strategy should also be interdisciplinary (not program by program). Developing an implementation strategy creates an important opportunity for continued collaboration with the public, Tribes, state and local governments, and other Federal agencies. [BLM H-1601-1 Land Use Planning Handbook, Section IV. A. (March, 2005)]

LCC: The 22 Landscape Conservation Cooperatives have been established nationwide by the Department of the Interior (DOI) to better integrate science and management to address climate change and related issues.

Objects and Values: The use of the term "objects" appears in the *American Antiquities Act of 1906* signed by Theodore Roosevelt which gives the President of the United States authority "…to declare by public proclamation historic landmarks, historic and prehistoric structures, and other objects of historic or scientific interest that are situated upon the lands owned or controlled by the Government of the United States to be national monuments…" The term "values" is presented in the *Omnibus Public Lands Management Act of 2009* and often in the establishing legislation for individual NLCS units. Throughout this document, the terms "NLCS resources," "NLCS values," or "NLCS resources and values" are used in reference to NLCS objects and values.

Stakeholder: An all-encompassing term which includes a person, group, organization, elected official, or government agency interested, affected or can be affected by an organization's action.

Sustainable Recreation: Recreational activities that provide for environmental sustainability while fulfilling social and economic needs of present and future generations of Americans.

Youth Program: BLM's Youth Program features 3 main components: School Age Programs, Youth Corps and Internships and Entry Level Careers. Focusing on youth from early childhood through young adulthood, BLM youth programs build upon childhood wonder of the natural world, provide hands-on-education and volunteer experiences that develop into long term engagement and stewardship and possibly careers.

http://www.blm.gov/wo/st/en/prog/more/blms_youth_initiatives.html